Rooted in Grace

A Bible Study for Finding Peace and Growth
while Planted in God's Unchanging Grace

By Rachel C. Williams

Hello,
Friends

In the middle of life's storms, where the ocean's waves crash and the winds howl, there is a quiet resilience found in the delicate wildflowers that bloom on the shore. These wildflowers, though small and seemingly fragile, are deeply rooted, flourishing where the sand meets the sea. They stand as a testament to God's sustaining power, growing in places where one might least expect.

"Rooted in Grace" is a 5 week devotional designed to guide you through a spiritual journey that mirrors this beautiful imagery. Just as these wiildflowers anchor themselves firmly in the shifting sands, this study will help you anchor your faith in Christ, allowing you to thrive even in the face of life's challenges. Drawing from the powerful symbolism of the ocean and the enduring strength of wildflowers, each week offers reflections, scripture, and practical applications to deepen your faith and cultivate a peace that can withstand any storm.

Join me. May your faith be rooted and your spirit blossom in the peace that only he can provide. I can't wait to get started.

xoxo, Rachel

Introduction
ROOTED IN GRACE

Hi, friends. My name is Rachel Williams and I am so incredibly excited to share a little of my story with you. I find myself feeling closer to God in nature, I always have. The beach specifically, holds a very special place in my heart. There is something incredibly calming about the sound of waves crashing against the shore, the sun on my face, and the sand beneath my feet. It's my go-to place for finding solace and peace amidst the daily challenges that come with living in this fallen world. Join me on this journey of faith, family, and the healing power of our Lord Jesus. Together we'll discover the strength that comes from the beauty that surrounds us every day, and the anchor of our soul that is Jesus.

Week 1

SETTING SAIL

Opening reflection: Let's embark together on a profound journey as we set sail into the vast ocean of God's grace. Like a ship preparing to navigate new waters, it's essential to anchor our hearts in faith. As wildflowers bloom along the shoreline, rooted deeply despite the shifting sand, we too must root ourselves in Christ as we face life.

Reflecting on Your Journey:
Before we jump into this session, let's take a moment for self-reflection. Consider the following questions as a way to connect your own journey to the metaphor of setting sail:

How will you rate the following? 1 being strongly disagree, 4 being strongly agree.	1	2	3	4
I can relate to the idea of life's challenges as an ocean, with waves of trials and seas of joy.	○	○	○	○
I feel equipped with tools to see God's grace even when the storms come.	○	○	○	○
I believe in God's goodness in all stages of my life, even when it's hard.	○	○	○	○
I am eager to learn how the ocean's metaphor can deepen my understanding of God's grace.	○	○	○	○
I am willing to dig into the word in order to deepen my faith.	○	○	○	○

Day 1- the ocean as a metaphor

Psalm 107: 23-32

Introduction:

Welcome to the first session of our Bible study, "Rooted in Grace": as we find peace and growth through God's unchanging grace. We begin this journey by setting sail, using the metaphor of the ocean to explore the challenges and triumphs of life. And just as the ocean is vast and unending, so is God's love for us.

The Ocean's Majesty:

Take a moment to picture the vastness of the ocean—the endless horizon, the gentle ebb and flow of the waves, and the boundless depths beneath the surface. The ocean is a reflection of life itself, often serene and beautiful, yet at times tumultuous and very overwhelming.

Life's Journey:

Just as sailors embark on their voyages, we, too, navigate the voyage of life. Our journey is marked by diverse experiences, including moments of calm and moments of turbulence. These experiences shape us, challenge us, and ultimately define who we are.

Psalm 107:23-32 paints a vivid picture of those who "went down to the sea in ships." This passage captures the essence of the ocean as a metaphor for life's journey. Like those who sailed the sea, we embark on a voyage, sometimes through calm waters, and at other times, through storms. In this metaphor, the ships represent our lives, and the sea represents circumstances and experiences surrounding us.

If you are reading this book, you may be feeling that you are in the middle of the rough seas that are causing you to feel overwhelmed. I vividly remember the first few weeks after my cancer diagnosis. I remember feeling very alone, even though I was surrounded by the people I loved most. I felt like there was no one that truly understood my exact situation. And honestly, I was scared and I had no idea what to do with the thoughts that I was having.

In this study, we will discuss practical and Biblical ways to take our thoughts captive, and truly live in the midst of the choppy waters. You are loved, sweet friend. Never forget that.

Reflection Question: How can the ocean, with its vastness and unpredictability, serve as a metaphor for the journey you've undertaken in a particular area of your life? What emotions and thoughts does this comparison evoke in you?

"In their distress, they cried out to the Lord."

Day 2- Understanding Grace

What is Grace?

Grace is one of those profound words that we often hear in the context of our faith, but what does it truly mean, especially in the midst of life's choppy waters?

Defining Grace

Grace, in a biblical context, can be defined as God's unmerited favor and love towards us. It's a concept that is both simple and incredibly profound. At its core, grace represents God's unwavering love and kindness, bestowed upon us regardless of our actions, merits, or circumstances. It's a love that is not dependent on our performance but rather on God's character. Isn't that beautiful? Have you ever truly sat and thought about what it means to be loved so unconditionally? There's NOTHING that you could do to make God stop loving you. That's pretty powerful.

Grace is like the gentle ocean breeze that nurtures wildflowers along the shore, providing them with everything they need to flourish in unexpected places. Just as these delicate blooms rely on the unseen elements of air and water to grow strong, we too, thrive through God's Grace.

When life gets hard, we may sometimes find it easy to question why this trial has come our way. But in understanding Grace, we come to realize that God's love doesn't depend on the absence of challenges. It's a love that shines BRIGHTEST when we need it most, in our moments of weakness.

Reflecting on Personal Experiences of Grace:

Before we proceed, I'd like to invite you to take a moment and reflect on your life. Have there been moments where you felt God's grace? Maybe it was a time when you experienced unexpected kindness from a friend or stranger. Perhaps it was the strength you found in prayer during a difficult day. These are glimpses of God's Grace in your life.

For me personally, I remember the day that I was leaving the hospital after recieving my intial staging and treatment plan. I expected to fall apart. But to my surprise and relief, the oposite happened. I felt the most divine sense of peace leaving that place. I knew without a shadow of a doubt that God was with me. That, was Grace.

Think about moments in your life and remember them as we continue our journey. Grace isn't an abstract concept; it's something deeply personal, something that can be experienced in our everyday lives.

To dive even deeper into the idea of grace, let's turn to Ephesians 2:8-9, a passage that beautifully encapsulates the essence of Grace in our Christian faith. Please take a moment to read these verses and consider what they mean to you:

"For by grace you have been saved through faith. And this is not your own doing; it is the gift of God, not a result of works, so that no one may boast." (Ephesians 2:8-9, ESV)

These verses remind us that our salvation, our connection with God, is not something we've earned through our actions. It is a gift from God—a gift freely given because of His boundless love. In the same way, we can also experience His Grace in our everyday lives, especially during challenging times.
Throughout this study, you will see that I refer to life as "our" journey. This is intentional because I'm right in the trenches with you. I never want you to feel alone, friend. I've got you. God has got you.

Reflection Question: Take a moment to think about the definition and significance of grace in your own life. How has God's Grace been a guiding force in your journey through the challenges of life? Does understanding God's Grace give you peace?

Day 3- Stories of Grace

Overview:

In today's session, we will explore the stories of individuals in the Bible who faced adversity and discovered God's Grace to be more than sufficient in their trials. These stories serve as powerful examples of God's unchanging grace, reminding us that, just as He was with them, He is with us in our journey.

Job's Perseverance:

In life's most challenging moments, we often find our true strength. Job, a man known for his unwavering faith, provides us with valuable insights into endurance in the face of adversity.

Job's story is one of perseverance. He faced unimaginable suffering, losing his wealth, health, and loved ones. Throughout it all, he clung to his faith, saying, "The Lord gave, and the Lord has taken away; blessed be the name of the Lord" (Job 1:21). This powerful declaration summarizes Job's enduring trust in God, even when everything around him seemed to crumble.

As we navigate our own battles, we can draw inspiration from Job. His story reminds us that even in the darkest of times, our faith can be our anchor. It allows us to stand firm when our circumstances threaten to overwhelm us. We can root ourselves in the unshakable foundation that is Jesus.

Joseph's Resilience, Trusting God's Plan:

The story of Joseph in the Bible is a remarkable testament to resilience and unwavering trust in God's plan. His life was filled with trials, but through it all, he remained steadfast.

Joseph's journey took him from being his father's favored son to being sold into slavery, wrongly imprisoned, and eventually becoming a high-ranking official in Egypt. Through every twist and turn, Joseph held on to his faith and the belief that God had a purpose for his life. Go ahead and take the time to read Joseph's story in Genesis chapters 37-50. As you read, try to draw some parallels from obstacles that you are facing, to those faced by Joseph.

One of the most touching moments in Joseph's story is when he finally reveals his identity to his brothers. After all the pain they had caused him, he says, "As for you, you meant evil against me, but God meant it for good" (Genesis 50:20). Joseph's resilience was born from his understanding that even in the most difficult circumstances, God was working for his good.

In our battles, or everyday challenges that come with living in a broken world, we can draw strength from Joseph's example. We may not always understand why we face adversity, but like Joseph, we can trust that God always has a purpose. Through our resilience and trust, we can emerge from difficult times with a deeper appreciation for His guiding hand, and even stronger in the end.

David's Psalm of Hope:

David, known as the psalmist, had a remarkable ability to express his deep emotions and unwavering hope in his writings, even in the midst of life's trials. One of the most famous psalms, Psalm 23, embodies the essence of David's hope in God.

In the opening verse, he declares, "The Lord is my shepherd; I shall not want." This simple yet profound statement reveals David's trust in God's provision and care.

David paints a vivid picture of God as a shepherd, leading His sheep to green pastures and quiet waters. Even in the "valley of the shadow of death," David fears no evil, for he knows that God is with him. The psalm concludes with the hopeful declaration that goodness and mercy will follow him all the days of his life.

In times of difficulty and uncertainty, we can draw inspiration from David's Psalm 23. It reminds us that, like a loving shepherd, God provides for our needs, offers us rest, and guides us through life's challenges. Our hope can rest in the knowledge that, just as David trusted God, we too can find strength and assurance in our faith.

Day 4- Setting Sail with Faith

Life is a journey, and our faith is the sail that carries us through its ever-changing seas. Just as a ship sets sail to explore new horizons, we embark on our path of faith with hope and trust in the One who guides our way.

Matthew 14:29 (NIV) "Come," he said. Then Peter got down out of the boat, walked on the water and came toward Jesus.

In this passage from Matthew, we witness a powerful moment when Peter walks on water toward Jesus. His faith compelled him to step out of the boat and set sail into the unknown. But as he looked at the stormy sea around him, fear gripped his heart, and he began to sink.

Peter's experience is a reflection of our own faith journeys. Sometimes, God calls us to step out of our comfort zones, to venture into uncharted waters, or to embark on something scary. These moments can be filled with uncertainty and fear, much like setting sail into an unpredictable ocean.

However, the key to success in this journey is faith. Peter remained buoyant and walked on water as long as he kept his focus on Jesus. The moment he allowed fear to consume him, he began to sink. The message is clear: when we keep our faith anchored in the Lord, we can set sail on even the most tumultuous seas.

Maybe you've already set sail on a journey filled with challenges and uncertainties. But remember, like Peter, your faith is the sail that will carry you through. Trust that God is with you, and when the storms of fear and doubt arise, fix your eyes on Him. Take intentional steps to take your thoughts captive and deliberately turn them to gratitude.

Just as the sea stretches out to the horizon, your faith can take you beyond the limits of your circumstances. Through your faith, you can walk on water, defying the odds and the expectations of the world! Trust in God's guidance, even when the waters seem rough. He will be your anchor and your compass.

So, as you set sail today, keep your faith in God at the forefront. Let it be the wind in your sails, propelling you forward. Don't be afraid to step out of the boat, because you are not alone. Together, we navigate the seas, anchored in God's grace.

Prayer: Dear Lord, as I set sail on this challenging journey, help me to keep my faith in You unwavering. When the storms of fear and doubt arise, let my focus remain on You. Be my anchor, my guide, and my strength. In Your name, I pray. Amen.

"Peter got out of the boat, walked on the water and came towards Jesus."

Day 5- Casting off
with Hope

"Be strong and take heart, all you who hope in the
LORD."
Psalm 31:24 (NIV)

Throughout this week, we've explored the metaphor of setting sail
on life's unpredictable and sometimes stormy seas. Today, as we
conclude this first week of our journey, we anchor our spirits in the
profound hope that God provides.

Reflection: Take a moment to contemplate the concept of setting
sail from the safety of the shore into the vast, open sea. Life is
much like this journey – filled with unknown adventures,
unexpected storms, and times of calm. But regardless of what lies
ahead, it is the anchor of hope that keeps us steady.

Hope isn't a passive attitude; it's a resilient posture of the heart.
It's the unwavering belief that even in the midst of life's tempests,
the Lord is with us, guiding our ship through it all. Hope fortifies
our strength, fills us with courage, and allows us to face
uncertainty with a heart that remains unshaken.

Guided Prayer: Gracious God, as we set sail on the sea of life,
we entrust ourselves to Your faithful guidance. Our strength and
courage come from the hope we have in You. Just as sailors rely
on their anchors in the midst of the storm, we anchor ourselves in
the certainty of Your love and presence. In Jesus' name, we find
our eternal hope. Amen.

Reflection & Discussion

Your Life's Voyage: How do you perceive your life's journey? Can you identify moments when you've set sail into the unknown?

Challenges at Sea: Have you faced challenging or turbulent times in your life that felt like stormy seas? What were these challenges,

Seeking Divine Guidance: During difficult moments, have you turned to Faith and God for support and guidance? How has your faith influenced your ability to overcome life's challenges?

Understanding God's Grace: What does the concept of God's grace mean to you, especially in the context of this particular challenge? How might God's grace be a source of hope and strength for you?

Heavenly Father,

As we begin this study and consider the concept of grace, we come humbly before You. Your grace is beyond our comprehension, yet it's a gift that we are invited to experience in our daily lives. We acknowledge that, in the face of life's trials, Your grace becomes even more precious.

We're grateful for the grace that saved us; it's not of our own doing but a beautiful gift from You. As we face the challenges of life, help us to grasp the depth of Your unmerited favor and love. Let it fill us with the understanding that Your love is not conditional, dependent on our circumstances, or our own efforts.

Lord, we remember moments when we felt Your grace. In unexpected acts of kindness, in moments of unexpected strength, and in the warmth of Your presence during difficult times. We hold onto those moments, knowing that Your grace is not a distant concept but a living, tangible force in our lives.

In the midst of this chapter, we seek a deeper understanding of Your grace. We pray that You reveal it to us in fresh ways, helping us to appreciate that it is not a theological notion alone but a reality that can provide comfort, strength, and hope.

Lord, remind us daily of Your grace. Help us to see it in the smallest acts of kindness, in the encouragement of loved ones, and in the peace that comes from trusting in You. May the understanding of grace empower us to stand firm in our faith, even when the storms of life rage around us.

We offer this prayer in gratitude for Your Grace in abundance. In Jesus's name, we pray.

Amen.

Week 2

NAVIGATING THE STORM

Opening Reflection: These self-reflection questions are designed to help you explore your experiences with God's grace in the midst of life's challenges and trials. Use them as a tool for personal growth and to deepen your understanding of God's grace.

- Think about a challenging situation you've faced recently. What emotions and thoughts did you experience during that time?

- Did you reach out to God for support or guidance when you were facing that storm? How did your faith, or lack of, influence your response to the situation?

- Reflect on the people, support, or resources that came into your life during difficult times. Do you believe now that these were expressions of God's grace?

- Have you shared your story of overcoming a difficult situation with others? How do you believe your experiences can be a source of inspiration and hope for those facing their own storms?

Day 1: Grace in Adversity

"But he said to me, 'My grace is sufficient for you, for my power is made perfect in weakness.' Therefore I will boast all the more gladly about my weaknesses, so that Christ's power may rest on me."
2 Corinthians 12:9 (NIV)

In this first session of "Navigating the Storm," we jump into the concept of grace in adversity. Life's journey, much like a sea voyage, has its storms and challenges. But God's grace is like an anchor that holds us steady when the winds of adversity blow.

Consider the storms of life as turbulent seas, full of uncertainty and chaos. These storms can take the form of health challenges, relationship difficulties, financial crises, or any other adversity you may encounter. Or sometimes, like in my life, they all seem to hit at once! While facing these storms, it's so easy to feel overwhelmed, vulnerable, and weak. These are feelings that Satan WANTS us to feel. He's there whispering lies to your soul in order for you to feel that there is no hope.

BUT, you have Hope in Christ Jesus. Think about God's grace as your unshakable anchor during these storms. His grace is not a limited resource but an endless wellspring of divine love and strength. It's a reminder that in your moments of vulnerability and weakness, you don't have to rely solely on your own abilities. You can't! You lean on God's grace, which is more than sufficient for your needs.

It's in these times, the power of God's grace becomes evident. It's like the calm at the center of a storm, providing you with stability, peace, and a sense of assurance. By boasting in your weaknesses, you acknowledge that it's through these very vulnerabilities that God's power shines most brightly.

Furthermore, by recognizing that His power is made perfect in weakness, you can embrace adversity with a different perspective. Rather than fearing or avoiding challenges, you can approach them with the confidence that God's grace will transform your moments of weakness into opportunities for His strength to be revealed.

Isn't that encouraging today? The fact that you can face the hardest things, with almost a sense of excitement. Reframe your thinking into happy anticipation of what God is going to do in your life! Because as soon as you begin to look for the ways that He is moving, the ways that he is using your storm for good, you WILL see them, friends.

As you navigate the storms of life, always remember that God's Grace is sufficient, boundless, and steadfast. It's your anchor, your refuge, and your source of hope when the winds howl and the waves crash. The storms may come and go, but God's grace remains constant, unchanging, and always available to you.

Self-Reflection Questions:
Can you recall a specific moment of adversity in your life when you felt God's grace sustaining you? What did that experience teach you about His grace?

How do you typically respond to adversity? Do you rely on your strength, or are you open to receiving God's grace in those moments?

Reflect on the Scripture passage from 2 Corinthians 12:9. How does it speak to you in your current circumstances?

What practical steps can you take to remind yourself of God's grace when adversity strikes, and how can you extend that grace to others facing their own storms?

Heavenly Father, we thank You for the gift of Your abundant grace. As we face adversity, we remember that Your grace is more than enough to carry us through. Help us to boast gladly in our weaknesses, knowing that in them, Your power is revealed. Grant us the strength and resilience to navigate life's storms through Your grace. In Jesus' name, we pray. Amen.

Day 2: More Stories of Grace

In our previous discussion, we began to explore the idea of God's grace in the face of adversity. Today, we're going to delve deeper into this concept by examining another story from the Bible where God's grace shines brilliantly in challenging circumstances.

One of the most compelling stories of grace in the Bible is that of Esther. Her narrative unfolds within the Persian Empire, where she, an ordinary Jewish girl, would go on to play an extraordinary role in saving her people from annihilation.

Esther's story begins with her unexpected rise to prominence. After the Persian King Ahasuerus dismisses Queen Vashti, he seeks a new queen. Esther, a young Jewish woman living in the capital city of Susa, is chosen from a vast pool of candidates. Her elevation to the position of queen is, in itself, an extraordinary act of grace.

The plot thickens when the sinister Haman, a high-ranking official, schemes to exterminate the Jewish population within the empire. Upon learning of this plot, Esther faces a profound challenge. She must decide whether to risk her own life by revealing her Jewish identity to the king in an effort to save her people.

What makes Esther's story a profound example of grace is her courage, selflessness, and faith. She famously utters the words, "If I perish, I perish" (Esther 4:16), demonstrating a willingness to sacrifice her life for the sake of her people. In response to Esther's bravery, God orchestrates a series of remarkable events that ultimately lead to the downfall of Haman and the salvation of the Jewish people.

The story of Esther reminds us that God's grace operates even in the most perilous circumstances. It reveals how ordinary individuals, when called to do extraordinary things, can become vessels of divine grace, altering the course of history and ensuring the safety of their community.

As we explore more stories of grace, let Esther's journey serve as a testament to God's providence and the transformative power of courage and selflessness in the face of adversity.

Self-Reflection Questions:

How do you think Esther's story may have been different if she relied on her own strength and provisions?

Consider how you might encourage and support someone who is facing adversity today. How can you be a vessel of God's grace in their life?

Dear Lord, we thank you for the stories of grace and redemption found throughout the Bible. Help us to see your hand at work in our own lives, even in the midst of trials and adversity. Just as you were with Esther, we trust that you are with us, guiding us through life's storms with your boundless grace.

Just as Esther stood resilient and beautiful amindst the trials, like a wildflower blooming in the storm, grant us courage and grace to thrive in our challenges. May we, too, reflect your strength and beauty through every trial.

Amen.

Day 3- Holding Fast in the Storm

Day 3 of our study is all about resilience, determination, and faith in the midst of life's storms. While we all wish for calm seas and clear skies, the reality is that storms will come.

In the heart of storms, we can find inspiration in the life of the apostle Paul. He experienced literal and metaphorical storms, enduring shipwrecks, imprisonment, and persecution. Paul's resilience in the face of adversity can teach us valuable lessons.

One of the most renowned stories is the shipwreck on the island of Malta (Acts 27). The ship he was on was caught in a powerful storm, and for two weeks, it was battered by the winds and waves. The crew had given up hope, but Paul, guided by his unwavering faith, encouraged them to stay strong. An angel appeared to him, assuring him that everyone on the ship would survive.

Through this story, we understand the importance of holding fast to our faith when the storm rages. Paul's faith was unshakable, and it gave him the strength to guide and encourage others. We are reminded that even in the darkest of times, our faith can be a guiding light for ourselves and those around us.

So, as we reflect on Paul's remarkable journey through life's storms, let us ponder our own sources of strength and resilience. What anchors us during challenging times? How does our faith enable us to hold fast when the waves crash in? These questions will guide us as we seek to cultivate unwavering faith in our own lives.

This day's lesson encourages us to find our spiritual anchor, to trust that God's promises are steadfast, and to navigate the storms of life with resilience and grace, just as Paul did.

Heavenly Father,

As we journey through the story of Paul and the tempestuous seas, we are reminded of the storms that occasionally rage in our own lives. Just as Paul faced turbulent waters, we too encounter challenges and uncertainties. In these moments, we turn to You for strength and resilience.

Lord, like Paul, we desire the faith and determination to hold fast when the storms threaten to overwhelm us. Grant us the wisdom to anchor ourselves in Your promises, for they are unshakable and unwavering.

We pray for the courage to be a source of encouragement and inspiration to those around us, just as Paul was to his fellow travelers. May our faith shine brightly even in the darkest of times, guiding others through their storms.

Lord, help us find strength in adversity and endurance in the face of life's trials. We trust that Your love and grace will sustain us, just as it sustained Paul during his journey.

In Your name, we pray.
Amen.

Day 4- God's Grace in the Darkest Hour

As we journey through a life in a fallen world, there are moments when we find ourselves in the deepest and darkest of hours. These are the times when despair threatens to overwhelm us, and we question where to find light in the midst of such darkness. For me, these times seem to occur when I am at home by myself with nothing to occupy my mind. I love to stay busy in order to ward times like these off. However, even when intentional, these days and times still happen. Today, we jump into the profound concept of God's grace in these darkest hours, discovering that His grace is not just a glimmer but a radiant beacon that guides us through.

What is most important during these times, is that we do not allow ourselves to stay here. We cling to God's truths in order to physically pull ourselves out of these times, because Satan is darkness, and Jesus IS LIGHT.

"The Lord is close to the brokenhearted and saves those who are crushed in spirit."

In the most challenging times, it's easy to feel distant from God, as if He is far away or has abandoned us. Yet, this scripture reminds us that God is closest to those who are brokenhearted and crushed in spirit. In your darkest hour, God's grace is a lifeline, pulling you close and guiding you to safety.

God's Grace Unveiled:

In times of great distress, God's grace may reveal itself in subtle but profound ways. It can manifest through:

- Unexplained peace: When turmoil surrounds you, you may find a sense of peace that defies logic. It's a peace that transcends understanding, providing solace in the storm.

- Strength amid weakness: God's grace empowers you to endure, even when you feel at your weakest. It's a supernatural strength that enables you to persevere.

- A community of support: Sometimes, God's grace is found in the kindness and support of others. They become instruments of His grace, extending love and care when you need it most.

- Revelations of purpose: In the darkness, you may discover a new sense of purpose or a deeper understanding of your calling. God's grace can use your trials to reveal His plan for your life.

I remember very well, the day that I received the cancer diagnosis and treatment plan. As my husband and I were walking to the car, I had the most overwhelming sense of peace wash over me. I audibly heard God whisper to my soul that it was going to be ok.

When you find yourself in your darkest hours, it's essential to have actionable tools to help you navigate through the difficulties and seek the light. Here are some tools you can use:

Prayer: Turn to prayer and meditation to find solace and connect with God. Take time to reflect, seek guidance, and find peace in your faith. Remind yourself of the Truths of God's word and repeat those truths in your heart over and over again.

Community and Support: Reach out to your support network, whether it's family, friends, a support group, or your church community. Don't be afraid to lean on others for emotional support, encouragement, and practical help. I cannot count the times that I have relied on my support system to get me through a particularly rough time. They WANT to help. Lean on them.

Journaling: Express your thoughts and feelings through journaling. Writing can be a therapeutic way to process your emotions, gain clarity, and document your journey. I have to admit, I used to feel that journaling was not worth making time for. But it has been through journaling that I have been able to put my feelings into words and allow those words to be dealt with between myself and God.

Reflection Questions:
1. Have you ever experienced a moment when you felt closest to God during a challenging time?

2. How have you seen God's grace manifest in your life during your darkest hours?

3. Think about a time when someone extended grace to you through their actions. How did it impact your life?

4. In your current challenges, can you identify any signs of God's grace at work?

Prayer: Dear Lord, in my darkest hours, I trust that Your grace is my guiding light. I thank You for being closest to me when I need it the most. Help me to recognize Your grace at work in my life, even in the most challenging times. Amen.

Day 5: An Anchor of Grace

"We have this hope as an anchor for the soul, firm
and secure."
Hebrews 6:19 (NIV)

Welcome to the final day of our "Navigating the Storm" journey.
We've explored the concept of God's grace during trials and the
hope it provides in our darkest hours. Today, we'll focus on how
this hope becomes an anchor for our souls, firm and secure.

Imagine standing on the deck of a ship as it sails through a fierce
storm. The waves are crashing, the winds are howling, and it
seems as if the ship might be tossed about uncontrollably. In the
midst of this chaos, what keeps the ship steady and the crew
hopeful? It's the anchor, securely holding the vessel in place.

Likewise, in the stormy seas of life, we need an anchor, something
to keep us steady and secure. For us, that anchor is the hope we
find in God's grace. It's the knowledge that, no matter how
tempestuous our circumstances may be, we are not adrift; we are
firmly held by the promises of God.

As mentioned before, hope isn't a passive attitude; it's a resilient
and intentional posture of the heart. It's the unwavering belief
that even in the midst of life's storms, the Lord is with us, guiding
our ship through it all. Hope fortifies our strength, fills us with
courage, and allows us to face uncertainty with a heart that
remains unshaken.

As we reflect on the anchor of grace, consider these questions:

- How has hope in God's grace served as an anchor in your life during difficult times?

- In what ways can you remind yourself of this anchor when facing storms of adversity?

- Think of a specific instance when God's grace held you firm and secure. How did this experience strengthen your faith?

- What practical steps can you take to deepen your understanding of the anchor of grace in your life?

- How can you share this hope and security with others who may be struggling in their own storms?

Guided Prayer:

Heavenly Father, thank you for being our anchor in the storms of life. Your grace is our hope and security. We rest in the knowledge that we are firmly held by Your promises, no matter what challenges we face. Help us to keep our eyes on this anchor of grace, to trust in Your unchanging nature, and to share this hope with those around us. In Jesus' name, we pray. Amen.

With this, we conclude our exploration of "Navigating the Storm." As you face the challenges of life, may you always find hope, strength, and security in the anchor of God's grace.

Week 3

DROPPING ANCHOR

Opening Reflection: These self-reflection questions are designed to help you explore your experiences with God's grace in the midst of life's challenges and trials. Use them as a tool for personal growth and to deepen your understanding of God's grace.

- Think about a recent rough day that you had; when you may have felt lost, anxious, alone, etc. Did you reach out to God for support or guidance when you were facing those feelings? How did your faith influence your response to the situation?

- Reflect on the people, support, or resources that came into your life during that time. How do you believe these were expressions of God's grace?

- Consider the role of hope in navigating adversity. How did hope in God's promises impact your journey through this time? Or did it? How could you have reacted differently?

Day 1: The Unchanging Nature of God's Grace

Malachi 3:6 states, "For I the Lord do not change; therefore you, O children of Jacob, are not consumed."

This verse emphasizes the unchanging and steadfast nature of the Lord, providing a source of comfort and assurance for all of us. Just as an anchor holds a ship steady and is unmoving, so is our God unchanging. In a world filled with uncertainties, the unchanging character of God offers a steady anchor for our souls. His grace is unwavering, providing us with hope and security.

Consider how an anchor is heavy and firmly rooted in the seabed, preventing the ship from drifting away. Likewise, God's unchanging character is the solid foundation upon which we can place our trust. When life's trials and tribulations threaten to toss us to and fro, we find stability and security in knowing that God remains constant. He does not waver or shift with the changing tides of our circumstances.

It's always been a comfort to me to remember that, no matter how chaotic my life can get, and as it changes from day to day, God never does. He is sturdy, unmoving, and constant at all times. It's also important to remember that, just as an anchor, He never moves. So on days when He seems far away, we may need to think to ourselves... "who moved?".

Heavenly Father,
we thank You for the unchanging nature of Your grace. In a world filled with uncertainties, we find hope and security in Your steady character. As we begin this week, help us anchor our souls in the assurance that Your grace is always there for us. Amen.

Reflection Questions:

In the storms of life, I often feel adrift when ....

One aspect of God's unchanging character that brings me the most comfort is ....

In moments of uncertainty, my anchor of hope in God reminds me that....

I can apply the concept of God as an unchanging anchor by....

How have past experiences solidified my belief in God's unchanging nature?

Day 2- Choosing Hope

As we journey deeper into our study, the theme of hope becomes ever more central. Hope, like an anchor, secures our souls amidst life's choppy waters. Today, we'll explore the profound connection between hope and grace, learning how this steadfast hope can be the source of strength, even in the most trying circumstances. Like a ship anchored in a safe harbor, we will discover the peace and security that comes from placing our hope in God's promises.

Today, we will also find encouragement in anchoring ourselves firmly in the hope that transcends the storms, a hope found in the promises of God. It is in this hope that we discover the true essence of being "Anchored in Grace."

Psalm 71:14 (NIV) "But as for me, I will always have hope; I will praise you more and more."

In this verse, the psalmist, traditionally believed to be King David, conveys an unshakable resolve. His declaration, "as for me," emphasizes a personal commitment to hope and praise. This phrase suggests that despite external circumstances, the psalmist chooses to maintain a spirit of hope and a heart full of praise.

1. **A Choice of Hope**: The psalmist proclaims that he will "always have hope." This declaration underscores the deliberate decision to maintain hope, regardless of the challenges faced. It implies a conscious choice to anchor one's faith in God's promises and trust in His unfailing love.. no matter what!

2. **Praising Amidst Adversity**: The verse further expresses the determination to "praise you more and more." This signifies that, even in difficult times, the psalmist seeks to intensify his worship and gratitude toward God. Instead of allowing adversity to silence his praise, he acknowledges the importance of magnifying God's goodness. These moments for me, look like worship sessions in my car! Praising Jesus through song, even on my toughest days.

Overall, Psalm 71:14 serves as a reminder that we can choose hope over despair and praise over discouragement. It encourages us to stand FIRM in our faith, knowing that even in the most challenging moments, our hope in God's promises can continue to grow and sustain us.

- How does this verse, Psalm 71:14, resonate with your own journey?

- In challenging times, what specific actions can you take to choose hope over despair and praise over discouragement?

- Reflect on a situation in your life when maintaining hope and offering praise made a significant difference. What did you learn from that experience?

- Consider the phrase "praise you more and more." How can you intensify your praise and worship of God in your current circumstances?

- Think about your ongoing relationship with God. How can you nurture it and experience spiritual growth, even in the midst of adversity?

Day 3- Trusting in God's Promises

In our journey of faith, we've explored the grace that anchors us and the hope that sustains us. Today, we turn our focus to the promises of God, those assurances that provide us with strength, comfort, and unwavering trust as we navigate life's challenges. God's promises are our refuge and our source of enduring joy. As we jump into this day's lesson, we'll discover how His promises can be the firm foundation upon which we stand, unwavering and secure.

Let's explore a selection of God's promises in Scripture. By truly grounding ourselves in these promises, we can better understand the unshakable hope and joy that they bring.

- **God's Promise of Presence** - Matthew 28:20: Reflect on the promise that God is with you always, even in the midst of life's storms.

- **God's Promise of Peace** - John 14:27: Contemplate the assurance of peace that Christ offers, a peace that is different from what the world gives.

- **God's Promise of Strength** - Isaiah 40:31: Consider how God promises to renew your strength when you feel weary.

- **God's Promise of Healing** - Jeremiah 30:17: Meditate on the promise of healing and restoration in the midst of your specific challenges.

"For the specific purpose of our study, I want to really expand and unpack Jeremiah 30:17 because it's a specific promise that I cling to.

" I will restore you to health and heal your wounds,' declares the Lord, 'because you are called an outcast, Zion for whom no one cares.'" (Jeremiah 30:17, NIV)

In my life, Jeremiah 30:17 takes on a special significance. This verse is a beautiful promise of God's healing and restoration, especially during times of physical and emotional distress. Life's journey can be filled with physical and emotional wounds. The promise of God's healing and restoration offers profound comfort and hope. It assures me that, even when we may feel like "outcasts" or as if no one truly understands, God cares deeply for us. He is not indifferent to our suffering but is actively working to bring healing and restoration to our lives.

As we reflect on this promise in the study, we can find strength and peace in knowing that our God is a healer. We can hold on to this assurance as we face the challenges of all kinds, finding comfort in the knowledge that God's healing is not only physical but extends to the depths of our souls.

This verse reminds us that God's grace and promises are not abstract concepts but powerful, life-transforming realities! As we anchor ourselves in these promises, we can navigate the storm of life with renewed hope and trust in the One who declares, "I will restore you to health and heal your wounds."

Prayer: *Heavenly Father, we thank you for your faithful promises. As we navigate the storms or uncertainties of life, help us anchor ourselves in your assurances of presence, peace, strength, and healing. May we find unwavering trust and enduring joy in the knowledge that you are true to your word. In Jesus's name, we pray. Amen.*

Reflection Questions:
- Which of God's promises resonate with you the most?

- How have these promises provided you with strength and comfort?

- What other promises in Scripture bring you hope and assurance during difficult times?

I encourage you to find a promise that resonates with you, and write it on a sticky note or index card. Stick it somewhere where you will see it often like your bathroom mirror, cabinet where you get your coffee cup in the morning, or on your computer at work! Reflect on His promises over your life daily.

Day 4- Joseph's Story of Hope

In our journey to understand and embrace hope, we revisit the remarkable story of Joseph from the book of Genesis. Joseph's life was a rollercoaster of events, filled with trials and tribulations, yet his unwavering hope and resilience serve as a beacon of inspiration for us, especially in the face of rough waters.

Scripture: Genesis 37:3-4, 18-28 (NIV)
Now Israel loved Joseph more than any of his other sons because he had been born to him in his old age; and he made an ornate robe for him. When his brothers saw that their father loved him more than any of them, they hated him and could not speak a kind word to him.

They saw him in the distance, and before he reached them, they plotted to kill him. "Here comes that dreamer!" they said to each other. "Come now, let's kill him and throw him into one of these cisterns and say that a ferocious animal devoured him. Then we'll see what comes of his dreams."

But Reuben heard them and rescued him out of their hands. "Let's not take his life," he said. "Don't shed any blood. Throw him into this cistern here in the wilderness, but don't lay a hand on him." Reuben said this to rescue him from them and take him back to his father.

Reflection:
Joseph's life story is a testament to the power of hope and resilience. From being betrayed by his brothers and sold into slavery to enduring false accusations and imprisonment, Joseph's journey was fraught with adversity. However, his faith in God and unshakable hope sustained him through every trial.

Dreams of Hope: Joseph was known for his prophetic dreams, which foretold a future where his brothers would bow before him. These dreams were a source of hope and vision even in the darkest of times.

Forgiveness and Redemption: Despite the injustices he faced, Joseph forgave his brothers when they eventually came to him in Egypt, acknowledging that what they had meant for evil, God had turned for good. This act of forgiveness and reconciliation speaks to the transformative power of hope. Think about our cancer. God can take something so ugly and meant for evil, and make it beautiful!

Divine Providence: Throughout his journey, Joseph recognized God's hand in his life, even when circumstances seemed dire. His trust in God's plan was the bedrock of his hope.

Discussion Questions:

How can Joseph's story inspire you in your specific journey? Are there aspects of his resilience, faith, or forgiveness that resonate with your experience?

Consider the dreams and hopes you have for the future. How can you nurture and hold onto these dreams, even in the face of adversity?

The coolest part about this story to me, is that Joseph's life exemplifies the idea that hope is NOT the absence of adversity, but the belief that God's plans are GREATER than our challenges. Just as Joseph held onto his dreams and unwavering hope, may we too find hope in the midst of our own trials, trusting that God can turn our challenges into opportunities for transformation and redemption. Be on the look out for those, friends. You are sure to see them.

Day 5- Our Unchanging Friend

In our final day of exploring the theme of hope, we turn our gaze again to the unchanging nature of God. While the storms of life may shake us, we can find solace and hope in the fact that our anchor, our God, remains constant and unwavering! Let's revisit one of my favorite verses and unpack it a little more.

Scripture: Malachi 3:6 (NIV)
"I the Lord do not change. So you, the descendants of Jacob, are not destroyed."

Reflection:
The reflection for this day centers on the unchanging nature of God and how it serves as an unshakable foundation of hope in our lives during whatever trial or uncertainty we may be facing. This concept is pivotal in understanding the enduring hope that we find in Him.

1. God's Faithfulness: Throughout the Bible, we encounter stories of individuals who faced overwhelming trials. Yet, they held onto the hope that God was with them and that His promises would come to fruition. This faithfulness of God can be a source of hope for us as well. It's a reminder that He has been there for countless others, and He will be there for us in our journey.

2. Drawing Strength from God's Unchanging Nature: The knowledge that God does not change is a powerful source of hope. In a world where circumstances can shift, people can disappoint, and life can be unpredictable, God remains constant. His character, His love, and His commitment to His children are unwavering. This unchanging nature gives us the assurance that He is working for our good even when we can't see the full picture. Anytime I think about this concept, I am always

reminded of the days when I used to embroider ALL of my girls' clothes...Seriously, it was a problem. But if you see the inside of the shirt, it was a GREAT big mess! There's no way to really fathom that a beautiful picture lay on the other side. I feel that this is how we see our lives sometimes. Our present circumstances are the inside of that shirt; a mangled mess that we can't see the beauty in right now. But God sees the big picture! He sees the other side and he just wants us to fully trust in his unwavering love and divine plans for our lives. There's beauty on the other side, girlfriend, just hang on.

3. <u>Anchor for Our Souls:</u> Just as a ship relies on its anchor to stay steady in the midst of a turbulent sea, we can drop our anchor of hope in the unchanging character of God. In times of uncertainty, pain, and fear, this anchor keeps us grounded. It allows us to withstand the storms of life with resilience and unwavering trust. Even when everything else feels like it's shifting, we have the reassurance that God remains the same.

In our lives, knowing that God is the same God who walked with Abraham, gave Joseph dreams of hope, and held David in his darkest hours provides comfort and strength. His promises are not empty; they are fulfilled in the lives of those who trust in Him. His love endures, and His character is a steadfast anchor.

I love the song by Elevation Worship, 'Same God'. It reminds us that His love endures through generations. The SAME GOD that moved in power then still moves in power now!

By reflecting on God's unchanging nature and discussing how it impacts our lives, we deepen our understanding of the hope that is anchored in Him. This reflection encourages us to find solace in His consistency, to trust that His plans for us are good, and to embrace the unchanging anchor of hope as we navigate the challenges that this life throws at us.

Discussion:

- Reflect on the ways God has been consistent and faithful in your life. Are there moments when you've felt His presence or seen His faithfulness in action?

- How does the knowledge of God's unchanging nature provide you with hope in your current season of life?

- Consider what it means to have an anchor of hope in God. How can you rely on His unchanging character to navigate life's storms?

As we close this week of hope, may we hold fast to the unchanging anchor that is our God. Just as the ocean's depths are unaltered by the storms on its surface, just as the wildflowers remain steadfast with deep roots despite the storms above, so too can we find hope in the unchanging nature of our Creator. Just as His promises endure, His love remains steadfast, and His presence is a source of unwavering hope for us, WE are anchored in His grace, and it is enough.

Week 4

EMBRACING GRACE IN DAILY LIFE

Opening Reflection: This week, we'll explore the practical application of God's grace in our everyday routines. As christian women, our faith journey extends into every aspect of our lives, and it's crucial to understand how grace can influence our choices, actions, and relationships. Let's embark on this week's lessons with open hearts and a desire to grow in God's grace.

Heavenly Father,

As we enter into this week of our journey, we come before You with open hearts and humble spirits. We thank You for the grace that has carried us through every and for the hope that sustains us.

Lord, as we explore the practical aspects of Your grace in our daily lives, we ask for wisdom and understanding. Help us to see Your grace at work in our choices, actions, and relationships. May we find strength and inspiration in the knowledge that Your grace is unending and ever-present.

Prepare our hearts, Lord, to embrace Your grace and reflect it in our daily routines. May we be a beacon of Your love to those around us. In Jesus' name, we pray.

Amen.

Day 1: The Grace-Filled Mindset

Scripture: Romans 12:2 (NIV) *"Do not conform to the pattern of this world, but be transformed by the renewing of your mind. Then you will be able to test and approve what God's will is—his good, pleasing and perfect will."*

Welcome to "Embracing Grace in Daily Life." This week, we jump into how you can practically apply a grace-filled mindset to transform your daily experiences. Our scripture today reminds us that we need not conform to the patterns of this world. Instead, we can renew our minds to discern God's perfect will, which is good, pleasing, and perfect.

I have found that, too often, we find ourselves swept up in the noise and distractions of the world-constantly pulled in different directions by societal expectations, worries, and the demands of everyday life. But God calls us to something deeper. He invites us to step away from the chaos and lean into His transformative grace. This transformation starts within, through the renewing of our minds. When we align our thoughts with God's truth rather than the shifting of standards of the world, we can experience a profound peace and clarity that allows us to walk confidently in His will. This renewal isn't just a one-time event, but a daily practice of surrender and trust, letting God's grace shape how we think, act, and respond in every situation.

Reflection: Let's think about how this grace-filled mindset can make a tangible difference in your daily life. How often do you catch yourself conforming to worldly patterns in your thoughts and actions? Can you identify areas where you might replace judgment, bitterness, or fear with compassion, forgiveness, and hope?

As stated before, Grace isn't just an abstract concept. It's a powerful force that can change the way you think, feel, and interact with the world. As you progress through this week, focus on the practical applications of renewing your mind with grace. Consider how grace can guide your responses, improve your relationships, and bring light into everyday situations.

Reflection Questions:

1. Can you recall a recent interaction where you found it challenging to extend grace to someone? What practical steps can you take to respond with more grace in similar situations?

2. In your daily life, are there specific areas or relationships where you tend to struggle with impatience, frustration, or judgment? How might recognizing and embracing God's grace help transform your approach in these situations?

3. Think about someone in your life who consistently displays grace in their actions and words. What qualities or habits do they possess that you could learn from and apply in your own relationships and daily life?

These questions can guide your reflections on extending grace in relationships, offering valuable insights into how you can live grace in your everyday interactions.

Day 2- The Grace of Forgiveness

Colossians 3:13 (NIV) - "Bear with each other and forgive one another if any of you has a grievance against someone. Forgive as the Lord forgave you."

In our journey to embrace God's grace in daily life, today we focus on the essential aspect of forgiveness. Forgiveness is a powerful expression of grace in our relationships. Just as God has forgiven us, we are called to forgive others. When we harbor grudges and hold on to past hurts, it weighs us down and hinders the flow of grace in our lives.

This subject is hard for me, and I have to pray that God softens my heart regularly. For me, forgiveness is an intentional and palpable thing. I'm not perfect in this area in any way, so I will be working with you through this aspect of the study. This day's lesson explores the transformative power of forgiveness and provides practical applications in order for us to extend grace through forgiveness.

Reflection: Think about a situation or person in your life that you've been hesitant to forgive. How has holding onto that unforgiveness affected your well-being and your relationships? Reflect on the freedom and grace that comes with forgiveness, both in your relationship with the other person and within your own heart.

Practical Application: (I'll be doing this too)

- Identify someone in your life you need to forgive. It could be a friend, family member, or even yourself.
- Take a moment to write a forgiveness letter. Express your feelings and extend forgiveness as an act of grace. You don't necessarily need to send the letter; sometimes, it's a personal exercise for healing.
- Pray for the strength to let go of any lingering bitterness and for God to replace it with His grace and peace.

Forgiving others is an ongoing process, but it is a powerful way to embrace God's grace in your daily life and relationships.

Day 3- A Grace-Filled Perspective

Romans 8:28 (NIV) - "And we know that in all things God works for the good of those who love him, who have been called according to his purpose."

In Day 3 of our Bible study, we explore the theme of "A Grace-Filled Perspective." It's a powerful concept, especially for those navigating the challenging waters of life. While facing any hardship, circumstances can be incredibly daunting. But looking at life through the lens of God's grace can bring comfort, hope, and strength.

Reflection is a vital part of this day. You're encouraged to pause and contemplate the trials and tribulations you've encountered during your life journey. Reflect on these experiences, acknowledging the pain and difficulty they brought into your life.

But, here's the transformative aspect of this reflection: After recognizing the challenges, you are invited to search for the glimmers of light within the darkness. Consider the positive outcomes, no matter how small they may seem. Did you discover newfound resilience? Strengthened relationships with loved ones? A deeper sense of empathy and compassion? Or a more profound connection to your faith?

By focusing on these positive aspects, you are shifting your perspective to see the silver linings within the storm clouds. It's about recognizing that even in the most challenging circumstances, God is at work for your good. The verse from Romans 8:28 reassures us that all things, even the most difficult ones, ultimately serve a purpose when we love and trust God.

This shift in perspective is a grace-filled one. It enables you to find hope in unexpected places, drawing strength from your experiences and your growing faith. It's a way to journey through whatever battle you may face, with a perspective filled with grace and the belief that, in God's hands, all things work for your good.

Practical Application:

1. Take a few moments to journal about a difficult experience you've had recently. Then, write down any positive outcomes or personal growth that resulted from that trial.

2. Share your reflections with a friend or support group, encouraging them to find grace and hope in their own challenges.

3. Begin a "Gratitude Journal" in which you write down things you're thankful for each day, no matter how small. This practice can help you maintain a grace-filled perspective.

Through this practice, you'll develop a habit of seeing God's grace at work in your life, even during challenging times, and find hope and strength in the process.

Dear Heavenly Father,
As I reflect on my life's journey and the trials I've faced, I'm reminded of your promise that all things work together for good for those who love you. Help me, Lord, to shift my perspective from fear and despair to one filled with grace. May I see the positive aspects that have emerged from the darkness, even in the midst of my challenges.
Grant me the strength to continue this battle with unwavering hope, knowing that you are with me every step of the way. Thank you for your grace that sustains me and the perspective it provides. In Jesus' name, I pray.
Amen.

Day 4- The Grace of Contentment

Philippians 4:11-13 from the Bible says:

"Not that I speak in regard to need, for I have learned in whatever state I am, to be content: I know how to be abased, and I know how to abound. Everywhere and in all things I have learned both to be full and to be hungry, both to abound and to suffer need. I can do all things through Christ who strengthens me."

In the face of anxiety and worry, we often find ourselves yearning for something different, something more. But true contentment isn't based on our circumstances; it's rooted in Christ. I often find myself yearning for my life before cancer, wishing I could go back and do things differently. But in Philippians, the Apostle Paul reminds us and teaches us the secret of being content, regardless of our situations.

So many hardships can act as a storm in our lives, but just like Paul, we can learn to be content within it, finding solace in God's grace. The battles we face do NOT define us, but how we navigate them, seeking contentment, love, and faith, can be a testament to God's grace in our lives.

I believe in God's power through contentment and its importance as he writes our testimonies. I'm going to offer up a prayer for us, and then list several practical applications in order for us to walk this out in our daily lives.

Prayer: *Dear Lord, in the midst of our journey, help us find contentment in Your presence. Teach us to rely on Your grace and not our circumstances. In the storms of life, may we learn the secret of being content, trusting in Your strength. In Jesus' name, I pray. Amen.*

Practical Applications:

- **Embrace Gratitude**: Make a list of things you're thankful for. Start or end your day by reflecting on these blessings, fostering a heart of contentment.
- **Limit Comparison**: Avoid comparing your journey to others'. Recognize that everyone's path is unique. Instead, focus on your own progress and the small victories.
- **Mindfulness Practice**: Engage in mindfulness exercises to center your thoughts on the present moment. Mindfulness can help you appreciate what you have today, rather than what you don't.
- **Journaling**: Keep a gratitude journal where you write down moments of contentment and grace you experience each day. Reflecting on these entries can encourage a positive outlook.
- **Seek Support**: Connect with a support group or a friend who understands your journey. Sharing experiences and coping strategies can help you find contentment amid adversity.
- **Serve Others**: Acts of service can shift your focus from personal struggles to the needs of others. Consider volunteering or helping someone in your community.

- **Prayer and Meditation**: Dedicate time for prayer and meditation, seeking God's presence and guidance. Pray for contentment and the strength to accept your circumstances.
- **Celebrate Small Victories**: Recognize and celebrate your achievements, no matter how minor they may seem. Each step forward is a triumph.
- **Lifestyle Choices:** Take care of your physical and emotional well-being through regular exercise, a balanced diet, and self-care practices that contribute to overall contentment.
- **Express Gratitude**: Express your thankfulness to loved ones who support you in your breast cancer journey. Let them know how their presence brings contentment to your life.

Remember, finding contentment in your life journey is an ongoing process. By practicing these applications, you can experience the grace of contentment, even amid the storm. I, too will be practicing these steps becaue I am FAR from perfect.

Day 5- Everlasting Grace

As we conclude this week on "Embracing Grace in Our Daily Lives," let us remember the beautiful metaphor of the ocean. Just as the waves continually touch the shore, God's grace washes over us, filling our lives with His love and mercy. Our journey, like the ever-changing ocean, is marked by its ups and downs, but we are anchored in grace.

Reflection: Think about the ocean's tides. They come and go, just as the challenges in life do. How has God's grace been a constant anchor for you, helping you navigate the ebb and flow of your journey?

As we close this week, let's embrace the enduring grace that keeps us grounded, no matter the storms that may come our way. May you find strength and hope in God's unchanging presence, just as the ocean remains steadfast and faithful. Just as the wildflowers remain anchored on the shore, you too have an anchor in Christ Jesus.

Closing Prayer: *Dear Heavenly Father, we thank you for the grace that anchors us, for the constant and unwavering love you pour into our lives. As we journey forward, may we remember that we are anchored in your grace, just as the ocean is anchored to the earth. In both the calm and the storms, you remain our refuge and strength. Amen.*

Remember, just as the ocean is always connected to the shore, you are forever connected to the grace of God, a grace that never wavers. Stay anchored in His love, and your journey will always find hope and purpose, just as the ocean always finds its way back to the shore.

Week 5

PRAYING THROUGH THE STORM

Opening Reflection: As we emter into this week's study, we embark on a journey through the powerful practice of prayer, discovering how it can be our steadfast anchor in the midst of life's storms. Much like a ship that seeks refuge from turbulent waters, we'll explore the role of prayer in providing shelter, strength, clarity, peace, and unshakable hope during our most trying times. With the vast expanse of the ocean as our backdrop, let's set sail into the world of prayer and find the shelter we need to weather any storm that life may bring.

1. How has prayer been a source of strength for you during challenging moments in your life, and what insights have you gained from these experiences?
2. Can you recall a time when prayer provided clarity and guidance in the midst of a personal storm? How did this experience shape your perspective on the power of prayer?

Day 1- Finding Refuge in Prayer

"God is our refuge and strength, a very present help in trouble."
Psalm 46:1

As the theme of this book proves, life's journey often leads us through rough and stormy seas, where the waves of adversity and uncertainty threaten to overwhelm us. Just as a ship seeks the safety of a harbor during a storm, we, too, find solace and strength in the refuge of prayer. It's in these difficult moments, when we're confronted with life's challenges, that we discover the profound beauty and power of communion with our Heavenly Father.

Our anchor in the midst of life's uncertainties isn't made of earthly materials but of faith, hope, and heartfelt prayer. In Psalm 46:1, we find these comforting words: "God is our refuge and strength, a very present help in trouble." This verse reminds us that God isn't a distant deity who remains indifferent to our trials. He is our refuge, our shelter in the storm, and our unwavering source of strength when the world around us seems to crumble.

For me personally, prayer is a sanctuary of hope and resilience in the face of a daunting diagnosis, in the face of divorce, and single parenting. In the midst of the physical and emotional turmoil that these things bring, I look to prayer as my steadfast anchor, providing both comfort and courage. Through prayer, we can pour out our fears, our hopes, and our deepest desires to a God who listens and truly cares.

Today, let's take a moment to reflect on the role that prayer has played in your journey. Has it been your refuge in times of need? Maybe it's been a source of peace when your heart was troubled, or a beacon of hope when the future seemed uncertain. But maybe it's not been a part of your life and you have been trying to navigate this life without prayer. Either way, as we enter into this week's exploration of prayer, consider how your relationship with God through prayer has evolved, and the ways it has offered shelter and guidance during life's storms. Or consider ways that you would like to grow in your prayer life and how that could make a significant difference in the way you aproach situations.

Reflection:
Take a moment to reflect on the storms you've faced in your life. How has prayer provided shelter and guidance during these times? Share a specific experience when prayer was a refuge for you.

If prayer has not been a part of your life, have a serious conversation with God now. Just as you would a friend. Pour out your heart to Him. He desires an authentic relationship with you.

Prayer:
Heavenly Father, we come before You in gratitude for the refuge and strength that prayer provides. As we embark on this week's journey, help us to deepen our understanding of the power of prayer during life's storms. Teach us to turn to You, our refuge, when the waves of adversity threaten to overwhelm us. Amen.

Day 2- The Power of Prayers and Praise

"I will extol the Lord at all times; his praise will always be on my lips. I will glory in the Lord; let the afflicted hear and rejoice. Glorify the Lord with me; let us exalt his name together." Psalm 34:1-3 (NIV

In the middle of life's challenges, it's natural for our minds to be consumed by worries and concerns. We often find ourselves dwelling on the uncertainties and fears that come with difficult times. However, as we enter into today's lesson, we uncover a powerful antidote to this common human response – the practice of offering prayers filled with praise and gratitude.

The Psalmist's words in Psalm 34:1-3 provide us with a profound insight. By choosing to "extol the Lord at all times" and keeping His praise on our lips, we shift our focus from our problems to God's greatness. In doing so, we not only acknowledge His sovereignty over our circumstances but also invite His peace and presence into our lives.

Praise is a transformative force that changes our perspective. It reminds us of the countless blessings and goodness that surround us even during the most challenging moments. By offering gratitude to God, we intentionally choose to see the silver linings in our lives, no matter how dim they may seem. It's a conscious decision to acknowledge His faithfulness and the countless reasons we have to be thankful.

By doing this, we create a bridge to connect with God's comforting presence. Our praises become an invitation for Him to draw nearer to us, offering solace and reassurance. In praising Him, we find ourselves glorifying the Lord, which, in turn, invites others to join in our expressions of gratitude, fostering a sense of community even in the storm.

Prayers of praise and gratitude, even in the face of adversity, hold the power to shift our focus, strengthen our faith, and offer solace that transcends our understanding. As we embrace this practice, we discover the incredible ability to draw closer to God, knowing that His presence is a constant source of comfort and hope during life's storms. Take some time to write in your journal, naming things that you are thankful for. By doing this we are shifting your mind to gratitude and continuing to build those new pathways in your brain so that this thought process will become more instinctual and automatic.

Heavenly Father, thank You for carrying me through this day. As I lay down to rest, I release all my worries and burdens into Your loving hands. Help me to find peace in Your presence, knowing that You are in control of all things. Renew my strength for tomorrow and guide me with Your wisdom. Fill my heart with gratitude for Your constant love and care. I trust You with all that's ahead, and I praise You for Your faithfulness. In Jesus' name, Amen.

Day 3- Deep Roots & Steady Waters

""The Lord is near to all who call on him, to all who call on him in truth". Psalm 145:18

Today, we focus on prayer as our lifeline, connecting us to God's steady presence amidst the chaos of life. Like wildflowers that anchor themselves with deep roots, drawing nourishment even in harsh conditions, prayer roots us in God's love and strength.

The ocean may be turbulent on the surface, with waves crashing and tides shifting, but deep below, the waters are calm and undisturbed. This depth mirrors the peace we can find in prayer, a place where our souls can rest, no matter the storms around us.

Step one: Find your quiet place. Just as wildflowers thrive in their chosen spot, find a place where you can be alone with God. It doesn't have to be perfect- just a space where you can focus and be still.

Step two: Begin wtih gratitude: Start your prayer by thanking God for His constant presence, like the deep steady waters beneath the ocean's surface. Acknowledge His unchanging nature, which grounds you through every challenge.

Step three: Root yourself in scripture: Use God's Word to deepen your prayer. Refelect on the verse above. Let this truth anchor your heart, reminding you that God is always close, listening and ready to provide peace.

Step four: Pour out your heart: Like the roots of a wildflower seeking nourishment, reach out to God with your deepest concerns, fears, and hopes. Speak honestly and openly, knowing that He hears you.

Step five: Listen and rest: After you have spoken, take time to listen. Sit quietly, letting the calm of God's presence wash over you like the peaceful depths of the ocean. Trust that He is working in your life, even when you cannot see it.

Step six: End with trust: Conclude your prayer by affirming your trust in God's care, just as wildflowers trust the soil to hold them firm. Surrender your worries to Him, knowing He will keep you steady and at peace.

Prayer: *Lord, help me to root myself in You through prayer, finding the peace that comes from Your steady presence. Just as wildflowers stand firm with deep roots, may my heart be anchored in Your unchanging love. Amen*

Day 4- Blooming Faith

""The righteous will flourish like a palm tree, they will grow like a cedar of Lebanon; planted in the house of the Lord, they will flourish in the courts of God". Psalm 92: 12-13

This scripture paints a picture of resilience and growth, much like wildflowers that bloom by the ocean, rooted deeply despite the crashing waves. These wildflowers face strong winds and relentless tides, yet they continue to thrive because their roots are firmly planted. In the same way, when we root ourselves in God through prayer, we gain the strength to endure life's storms. Prayer anchors us, connecting us to God's steady presense and allowing our faith to grow even when the world around us in in turmoil.

Life's challenges may come, but they don't have to overwhelm us. When we stay connected to God through prayer and His Word, we can flourish, reflecting His beauty and grace just like those wildflowers by the shore.

As you face life, remember the power of prayer and the strength that comes from being deeply rooted in God's love. No matter what comes your way friend, YOU can bloom in faith and stand firm.

Prayer: Lord, help me flourish in faith, even when life's storms rage around me. May prayer root me deeply in Your love and presence, giving me the strength to stand firm like the wildflowers that bloom by the ocean. Amen

As we conclude our journey in "Rooted in Grace" we reflect on the profound lessons we've explored together. This study was designed to guide you through the uncharted waters of life, using the metaphor of the ocean to help you navigate life's storms. Throughout our voyage, we discovered the anchor of grace, the enduring hope found in God's promises, and the practical ways to infuse Grace into our daily lives.

Our journey began with "Setting Sail," where we established the ocean as a symbol of life's challenges and God's grace. In "Navigating the Storm," we encountered the trials that life can bring and explored stories of grace that inspire us to persevere. "Dropping Anchor" reminded us that hope is our anchor, firm and secure, and explored the unchanging nature of our God.

In "Embracing Grace in Daily Life," we discussed the practical ways we can extend grace to others and apply it in our everyday choices and actions. Finally, "Praying Through the Storm" reassured us that God's promises are available to us, taught us how to pray, providing security and hope in the midst of life's tempests.

Through each chapter, scripture, reflection, and discussion, (hopefully) we've deepened our faith and found strength, even in the face of the most challenging circumstances. This journey reminds us that, like a ship at sea, we are anchored in grace and equipped to face any storm. May the lessons we've learned continue to guide you, offering hope, resilience, and unwavering faith.

Just as the ocean's horizon stretches beyond our sight, your faith journey doesn't end here. It continues, ever expanding and deepening, with new adventures and discoveries on the horizon. May you always find comfort, peace, and strength in the boundless ocean of God's grace, knowing that you are never alone. I pray that you become rooted in grace and in the Love that is forever unchanging, and that you bloom right where He has planted you.

As we reach the close of this devotional journey together, my heart is full of gratitude for the time we've shared reflecting on God's word and His unwavering presence in our lives. My prayer for you is that the seeds planted through these pages continue to grow, nourishing your faith, strengthening your spirit, and guiding you through every season of life. No matter what trials or triumphs you face, may you always remember that God is with you, offering His grace, love, and peace. I encourage you to keep seeking Him in every moment, trusting in His perfect plan for your life. I send you off with my deepest blessings and best wishes, knowing that with God by your side, you are never alone. Keep blossoming, keep trusting, and may your walk with the Lord lead you to greater strength and joy each day.

About
THE AUTHOR

I'm Rachel Williams, a wife, mother of three beautiful children, and a former teacher turned passionate faith-writer. Life has brought its share of challenges, but throught it all, God has been my unwavering source of strength and peace.

I find serenity in the beauty of nature, whether by the water's edge, surrounded by wildflowers, or in the quiet moments of reflection in God's Word. These experiences have deeply shaped my journey and inspired me to share my faith through writing. As the founder of Wildflower Faith Co., I 'm committed to helping others find the same peace and strength in Jesus that I have discovered, especially in the midst of life's storms. Thank you so much for being here, friend.

STAY IN TOUCH!

FIND ME ON INSTAGRAM

Faith Rooted ~ Peace Found

The Wildflower Faith Co.

Made in United States
Orlando, FL
11 November 2024

53689304R00038